# HORROR OVERHEAD

# Horror Overhead

Richard A. Boning

*Illustrated by*

Gordon Johnson

## The Incredible Series

Dexter & Westbrook, Ltd., Baldwin, New York

*To*
*Griffen Bond*

Captain Pruss' blue eyes sparkled with pride as the *Hindenburg* was led from the hangar. As spotlights played along the giant airship, its silver hull gleamed through the mist. By now all other nations had given up dirigible travel as unsafe. But then no other nation ever owned a ship like the *Hindenburg*. It was inconceivable that anything could happen to it.

At eight o'clock on that Monday evening of May 3, 1937, the Captain gave the signal, "Up ship." In two days the *Hindenburg* would arrive at Lakehurst, New Jersey. Bands played. Passengers waved to friends fading below at the airport near Frankfurt, Germany.

As Captain Pruss guided the ship to the North Sea, he recalled the anonymous threats received by the German government about the airship. At first he frowned, but then he dismissed the threats from his mind. Who could harm the *Hindenburg?*

"A magnificent airship," Commander Ernst Lehmann said in tones of awe. With a start Pruss realized that Lehmann, who stood beside him, had read his mind.

Both men knew they were borne aloft by seven million cubic feet of hydrogen. But in a third of a century of German zeppelin travel, no passenger had ever been injured by a hydrogen explosion. And the safest ship of them all was the *Hindenburg*.

The giant airship was a luxury hotel in the sky. Passengers had their own cabins. In the galley were two tons of delicious food. Notes from the aluminum piano in the lounge tinkled merrily. Passengers settled down to enjoy the trip.

In the reading room Mr. and Mrs. Hermann Doehner watched their children at play: Irene, ten; Walter, eight; and Werner, six. They were the only children aboard.

Philip Mangone, a clothing manufacturer from New York, looked forward to describing the trip to his daughter, Katherine. Twenty-one-year-old Pete Belin, of Washington, D.C., was impressed with the promenade deck. Through low-lying windows he could occasionally see the lights of cities passing below.

In time the reading room became deserted. Passengers retired to their cabins for a sound sleep, secure in the knowledge that all precautions had been taken for their safety.

Everyone knew that no airmen in the world were as thorough as the Germans. Ashtrays in the smoking room automatically put out cigarettes if passengers forgot to do so. When a crew member went topside, he wore an asbestos suit. Even the fuel in the four diesel engines was safe. It would not burn if a match were tossed into it.

The first sign that this might be something other than a routine trip came the next morning. To avoid a storm the *Hindenburg* was forced to circle to the north.

"We will be delayed, but we should still reach Lakehurst on Thursday," Captain Pruss told the passengers.

They were not alarmed. Joseph Spah spoke reassuringly to Ulla, his Alsatian dog, which was penned in the stern of the ship. Spah had just finished a successful engagement as an acrobat at the Wintergarten Theater in Berlin. He was taking the dog home to his family as a gift.

To help the thirty-eight passengers forget about the storm, fourteen-year-old cabin boy Werner Franz made absolutely certain everyone was comfortable.

On Wednesday storms forced the giant zeppelin further north, but Captain Pruss assured the passengers there was nothing to worry about. Some of them gathered around the piano and sang. Others listened happily.

That afternoon icebergs were sighted far below. As Mrs. Leonhard Adelt recalled later, they appeared to be carved from marble.

At dawn on Thursday, passengers saw the coast of Nova Scotia below. Soon they were gliding down the American coastline.

"We are over Boston," a crew member reported. But it was difficult to see anything. The city was shrouded in fog. Later, Bostonians would recall hearing the drone of diesel engines overhead.

Soon the clouds parted and passengers could see Long Island approaching. Crew members piled up luggage in preparation for the landing. Excitement swept through the ship.

Leonhard Adelt, a professional writer, looked forward to a reunion with two brothers that he had not seen for thirty years.

Suddenly — disappointing news. Thunderheads were building up off the New Jersey coast. The landing would be delayed. But the disappointment of the passengers gave way to interest as the skyscrapers of New York City appeared below.

Trolley cars and automobiles stopped in the streets so that passengers and motorists could watch the giant aircraft cruise in lazy circles overhead. Tugs and liners in the Hudson River tooted a welcome.

Passengers waved to spectators on the observation platform of the Empire State Building. The building was so close that people on the platform could be seen snapping pictures. Many of them waved in return.

After an hour the ship flew south and passed low over Lakehurst. It was now late afternoon. Below were cars containing friends and relatives who had been waiting for the ship since early morning. With a sigh spectators watched the *Hindenburg* as it continued south and disappeared in the distance. Word had been received that thunderheads were still in the area. In spite of the fact that the *Hindenburg* was long overdue, waiting relatives, though tired and impatient, were not alarmed.

The wife and children of Joseph Spah, the acrobat, had driven in that morning after attending church services. Katherine, Mangone's daughter, was there with a group of friends. Also waiting were the parents of Pete Belin. Their son had just completed his studies in Paris, and they were looking forward to seeing him.

Perhaps the only anxious person at Lakehurst was Herbert Morrison, announcer for Radio Station WLS in Chicago. He was there to describe the arrival of the giant aircraft. It was not going to be an easy job. There were no celebrities aboard as there had been on other voyages. Later, Morrison would recall searching his mind for something exciting to say.

Waiting with a landing crew was Chief Boatswain's Mate, Frederick "Bull" Tobin, a veteran of the disaster of the *Shenandoah*, an American dirigible lost in a crash ten years before.

The 248-man landing crew stood ready to assist the aircraft to the mooring tower by pulling on guide ropes. In charge of the entire ground operation was Commander Charles E. Rosendahl, another *Shenandoah* survivor.

Finally, word was received that the wind had died down and visibility was good.

Passengers chatted happily as the ship approached the airport. Exactly seventy-six hours and thirty minutes had elapsed since the departure from Frankfurt. It was now seven-thirty, Thursday evening.

Newsmen set up their cameras in the twilight as they watched the ship approach. The dirigible was 150 feet in the air and nearing the mooring tower.

Herbert Morrison was describing the passengers, who were smiling and waving from the windows. He was trying to create as much interest as possible.

"The ship is approaching like a giant feather," Morrison announced.

Leonhard Adelt was searching the crowd for a glimpse of his brothers. Suddenly he was aware of a strange stillness. The people on the ground seemed to stiffen. There were no shouts. Everyone was silent.

Adelt had no way of knowing that the crowd below was staring up with horror as a tongue of flame crackled across the top of the hull. A member of the ground crew said later, "I knew then that the ship was doomed."

Suddenly the entire tail section seemed to explode. Morrison screamed, "It's burst into flames! Get the ------ it's crashing ------ terrible!"

The explosion was heard ten miles away. Strangely, the people nearby, especially those in the airship, barely heard it. Adelt described it as a light, dull pop, something like a beer bottle being opened. He looked toward the stern and saw a glow like the sunrise. Then he knew that the ship was on fire.

Up forward in the control room Captain Pruss felt a soft thud. At first he was confused. Then he heard the muffled roar — and the screams.

As the flaming tail began to drop toward the ground, the Captain's mind worked swiftly. To give as many people as possible a chance for survival, he did not attempt to keep the ship aloft. As the bow shot up, the passengers tumbled down the hallways and corridors toward the stern.

Flames roared 500 feet into the air. To the spectators and the landing crew, it appeared that there was absolutely no chance for anyone to survive.

Announcer Morrison clutched his microphone and in a horrified tone shouted, "It's bursting into flames and falling on the mooring mast!"

Tiny figures the size of ants tumbled from the dirigible.

"This is terrible!" Morrison cried, "This is one of the worst catastrophes in the world!" He burst into sobs.

"It's a mass of smoking wreckage. I can hardly breathe --- I'm going to step inside where I can't see it. Folks, I'm going to have to stop for a moment."

At the time he was only dimly aware of it, but he heard noises like insects whining past his ears. Later he would realize that these were exploding bullets from the small arms store of the *Hindenburg*.

Katherine numbly hoped that her father, Philip Mangone, would not suffer. Later she would recall telling herself, "He died quickly."

The parents of Pete Belin were stunned. Friends forced them back into their automobile, where they would not have to witness the tragedy.

As her children sobbed, Mrs. Spah screamed.

The ground crew could hardly believe their eyes. Above them was a flaming monster three blocks long. The heat beat down on them. In a matter of moments the raging inferno would come crashing down. Suddenly they began to scatter. Bull Tobin bellowed at them to return. The crew hesitated. Then they began moving back toward the roaring flames to assist any possible survivors.

Inside the ship people reacted instinctively. Mrs. Doehner picked up six-year-old Werner and flung him from a window. She then pushed Walter through. Irene had disappeared, looking for her father.

Leonhard Adelt urged his wife to a window. Later he would not recall how either of them got to the ground. Both he and Mrs. Adelt picked their way through the white-hot metal. As they broke through the wreckage, they started to run.

Adelt suddenly realized that his wife was no longer with him. Turning, he saw that she had fallen on the sand. He lifted her up and pushed her, and she began running like a mechanical doll that has been rewound. Then Adelt himself stumbled and fell. It all seemed like a dream. As he was losing consciousness, his wife returned and brought him to his feet. She led him by the hand like a child, and they both stumbled to safety.

Joseph Spah, the acrobat, had trouble opening a window. He battered the glass with his camera, and the entire window disappeared.

Two men climbed out past him and hung to a girder. Spah followed. One of the men fell kicking and thrashing to the ground — 100 feet below. Spah saw his body bounce when it struck the earth. Then the other man fell. As he did, he lunged at the acrobat, tearing the lapel from his coat. Grimly Spah clung to the hot metal. One of his best acts had been an imitation of a drunk hanging onto a lamppost. He would never need his skill more than now. Slowly the ship rose 200 feet and then gradually began to settle to the ground. It was still a long way down. But Spah could stand it no longer and released his hold. As he fell, he prepared himself for the shock. To this day, he does not recall striking the ground or dragging himself away from the awful heat.

Young Pete Belin had been taking pictures when the explosion occurred. He jumped, hoping that he might somehow survive.

Mangone was thrown to the floor by the explosion.

In the control room Captain Pruss and his crew were remarkably cool. They had done everything possible to give the passengers a chance to escape.

"Jump," ordered Pruss.

Crew members leaped to the ground below.

In the meantime, Mangone was pinned under the wreck. Fortunately, he was able to dig a tunnel under the moist sand to safety.

Incredibly injured persons were struggling from the wreckage. A man walked stiffly from the flames. His hair was singed and his face puffy. He acted as if nothing had happened. Although his flesh was charred, he talked calmly in German. Rescuers led him to an ambulance as he continued to speak. Once inside, he fell over — dead.

What about Werner Franz, the cabin boy? His experience was the most unusual of all.

When the first explosion occurred, he was dazed by the heat and unable to move. Fire broke out all around him. Without knowing how, he was finally able to stumble to a hatch in the bottom of the ship. Jumping through the open hatch, he was aware that the entire burning dirigible was descending on him. Dimly he knew that he was about to die.

Just as he was losing consciousness, a water tank burst and drenched him. The shock of the cold water cleared his mind. Protected by his wet clothing, he struggled through the burning ruins to safety.

Mangone was now arguing with rescuers. "My daughter is here," he said. "I must find her."

He was right. His daughter spotted him in the crowd. His hair had been burned off and his hands were bleeding — but he was alive.

Herbert Morrison, radio announcer turned rescuer, attempted to help Mangone into an ambulance. Somewhere in his Boy Scout training he remembered learning that a burned person should be held under the armpits. The flesh there is least likely to be burned.

The Air Station was now filled with doctors and nurses. Captain Pruss was badly burned trying to save others. But he would survive.

Hermann Doehner was nowhere to be found. His wife and three children were brought to the hospital. All were hurt, and Irene had only a few hours of life remaining.

In the meantime, Pete Belin's parents had given up hope. As they were about to drive sadly away, they heard a whistle that sounded strangely like their son's. As they turned, they saw him coming toward them. Miraculously, Pete had landed on a pile of soft sand and was completely unharmed. His suit was not even rumpled.

Mrs. Spah prayed and tried to calm her crying children. To prevent them from being run over by trucks and ambulances, she took them into the hangar.

As she stood there, she heard someone shouting, "Spah!" She was almost afraid to respond because she dreaded hearing the worst.

"Yes?" she asked fearfully.

"Your husband is all right," said a soldier.

She found Joseph sitting on a bench, dazed. He did not tell her that the pet Alsatian dog had perished in the flames.

Now just thirty-three seconds after the fires had first broken out, the giant airship lay in smoldering ruins. The death count had reached thirty-three, and four more were destined to die, including a member of the ground crew.

Commander Lehmann himself was mortally injured. He kept repeating, *"Das versteh ich nicht."* — "I can't understand it."